MARRIAGE UNCUT

II

Straight Talk, No Chaser

TENITA C. JOHNSON

 Published by So It Is Written, LLC
Detroit, MI
SoItIsWritten.net

Marriage Uncut II: Straight Talk, No Chaser
Copyright © 2019 by Tenita C. Johnson

All rights reserved. No part of this book may be reproduced or transmitted in any form or by any means, electronic or mechanical, including photocopying, recording, or by an information storage and retrieval system - except by a reviewer who may quote brief passages in a review to be printed in a magazine or newspaper - without permission in writing from the publisher.

Edit by: Shairon Taylor and Lita P. Ward

Formatting: Ya Ya Ya Creative – www.yayayacreative.com

ISBN No. 978-0-9904246-6-6

LCCN: 2019902520

PRINTED AND BOUND IN THE UNITED STATES OF AMERICA

OTHER WORKS
by Tenita C. Johnson

---

100 Words of Encouragement:
Tidbits of Inspiration

100 Words of Encouragement:
Tidbits of Inspiration – Audio Book

100 Words of Encouragement II:
Driven to Dream

When the Smoke Clears:
A Phoenix Rises

Grammatically Incorrect:
When Commas Save Your Sentences & Your Reputation

From Fatherless To Fearless

The Wait of Success:
How to Become an Overnight Success in 7,300 Days

Marriage Uncut: Straight Talk, No Chaser

Available at <u>SoItIsWritten.net</u> and <u>Amazon.com</u>

Table of Contents

Foreword 1
    About the Author: LaShun Franklin, MA & LLP 5

Hallmark Heartbreak 9
    About the Author: Angie Green 27

Hardwood Floors 31
    About the Author: Tenita C. Johnson 47

A Little Drama Goes a Long Way 51
    About the Author: Orlando Crawford 65

Wrong Turn Down Relationship Road 69
    About the Author: Natasha Crawford 87

Dr. Jekyll, Mr. Hyde 91
    About the Author: Coni Hookfin 111

About: So It Is Written 113

About: The Red Ink Conference 115

Foreword
by LaShun Franklin

Marriage. The oldest and first relationship designed in the earth, as we know it. The very foundation of most societies exists because a man and a woman made a choice (or it was chosen for them) to be in a committed relationship. In Western culture, we have many catch phrases that try to describe the journey of marriage. While some are positive, others are negative. However, what it all boils down to is this: *marriage is hard work!*

Many married couples spent more time dreaming about their lives together and planning a wedding than they did preparing for the new job description of husband or wife. Many of us had to figure *it* out as we went along, evaluating daily if the investment was even worth it! Many of our predecessors hid the work and presented to us a scripted look at marriage, which unfortunately could have never properly prepared us for what came next.

In Matthew 19:11-12, in the Message translation, Jesus has some "real talk" with the Pharisees and His disciples: *But Jesus said, "Not everyone is mature enough to live a married life. It requires a certain aptitude and grace. Marriage isn't for everyone. Some, from birth seemingly, never give marriage a thought. Others never get asked - or accepted. And some decide not to get married for kingdom reasons. But if you're capable of growing into the largeness of marriage, do it."*

Jesus clarifies a couple of things that people need to understand well *before* they enter a marriage. In verse 11, the key is that not everyone is *mature* enough to live a married life. In verse 12, He reiterates his message saying, "Marriage will *grow you up, if you're up to the challenge!"* This is not a negative statement; however, it is a very encouraging one. Jesus is encouraging us to examine our own capacity to love others and please God in doing so. The earlier verses in this 19th chapter support God's original plan for marriage and what standard He is expecting from those of us who choose marriage.

Marriage Uncut: Straight Talk, No Chaser is an "in your face" look at the real work of real marriages. It gives us a very raw and uncut look at the potential situations that every marriage may experience and the decisions that the writers chose when faced with these challenges. Reading this book feels like you are interviewing a couple on a scripted reality television show. Some situations may echo your own, or may mirror the lives of someone you know. You may find yourself laughing, crying or praying with and for these couples as they share their candid truths. The level of transparency may even feel slightly embarrassing, at times, but you will 'get it'! We get to witness the *maturation* and *expansion* opportunities that marriage offers, in the wake of personality differences, mistakes, trials and lack of knowledge.

Unfortunately, we do not currently live in a culture or nation that supports healthy marriage, like it did in earlier years. With a 50-60% divorce rate in the U.S., and the decline of the traditional family, we have to take a hard look at how we can help others make good, healthy decisions concerning marriage. In the many years of providing counsel and mentoring for couples, I have found that good preparation, tools, support and transparency is key to helping couples thrive. In the event that challenges occur during marriage (which they will), having transparent, mature mentors and accountability is golden! This anthology is not for the person who chooses to hide behind the face of religion or fantasy. The uncut nature of their accounts can be used as a teaching tool to provide readers with hope, insight and courage to make better choices in their own marriage.

I leave you with my life's motto: "Marriage is good. Family is good. Marriage is work, and it is a good work. Everything can be fixed, so let us get on with it!"

About the Author
➡ LaShun Franklin, MA & LLP

While many people choose to brush their issues under the rug, LaShun Franklin, MA & LLP, removes the rug altogether, helping clients deal with their issues head on. Realizing that it's often easier for people to hide behind the masks of guilt, shame and error, Franklin works wholeheartedly to usher her clientele into their purpose, passion and prosperity. Specializing in mood disorders, anxiety, ADHD, and grief, she teaches her clients that in order to effectively live, one must die to self on a daily basis.

In addition to holding a Bachelor of Science in Psychology and a Master of Arts in Marriage and Family Therapy, she is also certified as a Limited Licensed Psychologist by the State of Michigan and a Trauma and Loss Specialist. Her tenacity to help clients heal from past wounds, coupled with her educational background, opened doors for her to lead Facilitating Open Couple Communication, Understanding and Study (F.O.C.C.U.S.) and the Prevention and Relationship Enhancement Program (P.R.E.P.). Obtaining ministerial training from Rhema Bible

College, certification from Light University, and her license through Destiny Outreach Ministerial Alliance (DOMA), Franklin has made it her mission to restore broken marriages and families—one client at a time.

Serving as a master-level psychotherapist, she uses a wide variety of theory-based techniques, such as Cognitive Behavioral, Rational Emotive Therapy, Solution-focused Brief Techniques, Play-based Activities and Gestalt Psychology. Through her creative strategy efforts and out-of-the-box problem-solving techniques, Franklin helps her clients realize that success truly happens—not when you have all of the answers to life's questions—but when you are able to face the questions you've been avoiding your whole life.

Understanding that life is often driven by relationships, she coaches couples, families and individuals alike on how to set boundaries, sever ties with unhealthy relationships, rebuild self-esteem and live the abundant life the way God intended. As a master motivator, teacher and purpose coach, she is committed to helping her clients turn their worry and wounds into wisdom. And while many will tell you that time heals all wounds, she will argue that healing—true healing—only comes to those who are willing to peel back the layers and do the work.

For appointments or more information, please email lashun@songsofsolomonri.com or call 313-794-5152.

Hallmark Heartbreak
by Angie Green

When I think of the concept of having the "perfect" marriage, I imagine a marriage that shelters you from all the harms of the world. The marriage would be like a filter and life would be wonderful. Soon after meeting my husband, I thought I was well on my way to obtaining the perfect marriage. He entered like no other man had ever come into my life. He brought home-cooked food to my job and took me on a *real date* to see a Tyler Perry production. He came to my door like a gentleman (with flowers and candy). I greeted him with a smile and invited him in. He was patient while I finished getting ready. After we left the theatre, I thought that was going to be the end of our evening. To my surprise, we went out to dinner. When I looked at this man, my eyes were on the verge of saying things my lips shouldn't.

This was the beginning I had always envisioned. After we ate, we went back to my place. We continued to talk, getting to know each other better. Everything was going well. The conversation was flowing well until he caused it to come to a screeching halt.

"Do you know how much this date cost me?"

The well in my eyes dried up and my smile flipped upside down. "What did you say?" I replied.

It's funny how something so little could easily ruin a (seemingly) perfect date. To be honest, part of the reason that it bothered me so much was due to the fact that I wasn't truly feeling him initially anyway. But, after a wonderful date, he was growing on me pretty quickly. After reflecting on our evening, I gave him a chance to clarify his question. Seeing I was upset, he took my hand and tried to fix the mess he'd made so quickly.

"No! Don't take it like that. I was only saying that when you factor in the cost of the flowers, candy, date and dinner, that may be all you see. But there's more."

I shifted my position to hear what else he had to say.

"Where should I be at this time of day?"

Thinking about it, I said, "At work?"

"Right. I passed on 12 hours of overtime just to be here with you. The look on your face, and how you made me feel when I was with you, made that decision so worth it."

Houston, we no longer had a problem. I relaxed from my once tense state. My eyes welled up again and the smile returned. Optimism saturated my heart. Even though it took us months to go on our first date, it was well worth it. Each of us had a baby and our work schedules conflicted greatly at first, preventing us from dating.

We continued seeing each other; this time, employing more creative measures to make sure that we saw each other more frequently. Since he worked not far from my house, I often went to his job. Soon, we both dedicated our off days to each other. A few months later, it was obvious that we should take our relationship to the next level.

I got my first brand new car on November 3, 1999. When I told Jonathan, he asked, "Can you bring it up to the job so I can see it ...*and you?*" I granted his request. After congratulating me on my purchase, he wanted a hug. Once again, I granted his request. I was truly into this man. His embrace felt like life and it was much appreciated. Eventually though, my feelings started to betray me. Every time he held me, I wanted to go against my own promise: I promised to wait for Mr. Right before giving myself to another man. But, my flesh had thoughts of its own.

Before I left his job, he asked, "Since you don't work tomorrow, can I see you when I get off tonight?"

At 4 a.m. in the morning? I thought.

"How?"

When I looked up at him, I saw he had a house key in his hand. He asked, "Can you be there waiting for me when I get off?"

I had never done anything like that before in life. I wanted to say, "No" because I knew it was going to be more than *just seeing me*. My mind was saying one thing, but my body said another. The next thing I knew, his key was in my hand and I was saying, "Okay." I guess my body won. I wanted my next sexual experience to be after marriage. However, memories of our first date, the way I felt that day, and the way he treated me since made my decision easier.

Even though we had known each other for only six months, and actually dated for only two, we felt safe enough with each other to introduce our kids to each other. This decision for me was even easier because Jonathan had grown up with my best friend (and co-worker). She had already given me her stamp of approval. When we introduced our children to the relationship, my daughter Raven had just turned six, while his son was eleven. They really hit it off. My perfect marriage was beginning to become a reality.

On January 1st, we brought the New Year in by seeing a movie, which was a little different than what I was used to. But, it was enjoyable. Around March of that year, I found out I was pregnant with twins. I couldn't have been happier because I was truly in love with this man. Even though we had known each other less than a year, I didn't want to have any more kids outside of marriage. Yes, I was disappointed for the choices I had made leading up to this moment and I had no one but myself to blame. I had to find out how to tell this man I was now pregnant with two babies. I didn't have a clue as to how he was going to react. Was he going to accept this, or was he going to do what some men do and deny being the father before he ended the relationship? One thing was for sure. I couldn't wait too long because I was spending nights with him, so I couldn't hide my morning sickness.

Terrified of the unknown, I told him, "I've been feeling sick lately. I went to the doctor. He said that I was…"

Before I could finish, he finished the sentence for me. "Pregnant? Are you pregnant?"

Then, the biggest smile came over his face. He held me and I mustered up enough words to respond.

"Yes…with twins."

"Oh my God! That is wonderful!"

It wasn't the response I was looking for, but it made me love him even more. It mattered even less that we weren't married.

We decided to move in together, which was a huge step for me. I was so inexperienced at living with a man and Jonathan was ten years my senior. I felt loved and wanted by him. He was truly the man of my dreams. Upon reaching my second trimester, I started having issues with my blood pressure and hydration. When I became twenty-one weeks, I was admitted into the hospital. Soon after, my water broke, causing me to go into premature labor. My memories after that are faint. I remember giving birth to Jaila first, who came out silent. An hour later, I delivered Jalene, who was whimpering ever so slightly. I could hear her. I was hopeful that I was going to keep at least one of my babies.

Those hopes were shot down when the doctor said, "Because of severe dehydration and the water breaking, it caused infection to set in. At under twenty-five weeks, regretfully, there's nothing we can do for them."

We were both devastated. Jonathan still cries over the loss of our beloved daughters. I did thankfully get to hold Jalene for a while before her little heart stopped. I was so thankful that I did not have to go through this alone. I needed his support like never before. My mind was echoing with the nightmare of my first pregnancy:

I arrived at the hospital. Once my mother signed all the necessary paperwork, because I was underage, I was left alone. Sixteen years old, with no knowledge of what I was about to go into, I didn't have a parent or baby's daddy for support. I promised myself in that moment, "The next time I do this, I'm going to have a husband!"

After the miscarriage, we were informed that because the babies were born alive, we had to name them and arrange funeral services for them also. This became a huge nightmare for us both. In this short span of our great relationship, we were delivered a major blow. We weren't sure our relationship could survive it. After their burial, Jonathan and I were at home. He was in the kitchen cooking and, as I entered, I noticed him grieving heavily. That was the first time I had ever seen a man cry. Seeing him in tears was heart breaking. All I could do was hug him tightly and hope that we could get past the pain.

Months later, Jonathan and I were doing well. We were still mourning our daughters, but living through our grief. Jonathan and I decided to get married. I was so excited that things were starting to look up for our unexpectedly smaller family. I was just like any other newly engaged woman. My wedding had to be elaborate because this would be our first, and only time, getting married. I quickly went into planning mode. I wanted a beautiful ceremony, but I knew funds were limited. We picked a date that we thought would be perfect: Saturday, March 17, 2001. I was truly excited. That date had no specific importance, but it would to me once I said, "I do," to my new husband. After announcing the wedding date to our families, we started planning our special day. We had items personalized and we located a nice place for our wedding and reception. Everything was booked and ordered.

We were three months away from our wedding. I came home and greeted my soon-to-be husband with a customary hug and kiss. Afterward, he had a look on his face that was unfamiliar to me. He took my hand and led me to the couch. I wasn't sure exactly what was going on, but I sat next to him.

Emotionless, he looked at me and said, "I have to tell you something."

I immediately got this unnerving feeling. Jonathan looked at me again before continuing.

"I haven't been completely honest with you about a few things. So I need to tell you now. We are still getting married. Know that I love you and I don't want to hurt you by not telling you the truth anymore."

By now, I was upset. I still didn't know what in the world this man was about to say to me.

"I'm married."

I had a dumb look on my face. I knew I wasn't hearing what I thought I'd just heard.

"Married to who? Why would you start a relationship with me, living like you are single the entire time?"

He went on to tell me that he was married to his child's mother. They eventually separated, but never got divorced. Someone told him that he could obtain a divorce in 60 or 90 days. He was either misinformed or misunderstood, but in Michigan, it takes much more than 90 days for a divorce to be complete! Now he was stuck. He felt like it would be no harm, no foul, if he could get the divorce before we got married. His plan was that I would never have to know that his previous marriage ever existed. Now the tables had turned. After we got the correct information, we found out that it takes six months before a divorce can be finalized. His confession really made me look at him differently.

To me, he was a man who could do no wrong. He never lied to me. Then, I felt like I was truly in a relationship with a person who I didn't know as well as I thought. That was a hard pill for me to swallow. It was nothing I'd ever experienced before. My emotions were all over the place. I was so upset with him. I went from being so happy that I was marrying the man of my dreams, to being in a relationship with a man I fully didn't know. I couldn't look at him. I couldn't even speak. I was upset with him, but even more so, with myself.

I asked myself, *Was I that desperate to be in a great relationship that I ignored the signs?* When we got together, he was living a single life. No one close to him ever mentioned the fact that he was still married. Now, I felt like "the other woman" in this relationship. I saw these things on television, not knowing that I would one day be living this situation out in my personal life. My dreams for the perfect marriage were crushed.

After his confession, he explained his reasons why he never disclosed his prior marriage to me. But I was so upset that I couldn't listen to what he was saying. I believed some things; other things, not so much.

"You know I love you. I was afraid you would leave me. I wanted to tell you, but the right time just never came up."

I was an inexperienced young woman, who was head over hills in love with a man who had ten years of life over me. Jonathan was the first man to ever treat me like I felt a man should treat a woman. Was I living a fairy tale life based off *Lifetime* and *Hallmark* movies? Growing up, my parents didn't teach me all the things I should know about being a young lady because they didn't know themselves. You can only teach what you know or experience. So, they taught me what they could and they cared for me as best as they could. With little education in my family, I didn't have anyone in my circle who I could truly turn to about what I was dealing with. I eventually had to go outside my family and speak to a good friend about what I was dealing with. She didn't tell me exactly what I wanted to hear, but she was straight forward. That's what I needed.

Before I could recover from this "news" from Jonathan, I got laid off from my job. If it wasn't one thing, it was another! The wedding was put on hold. I didn't know if I would ever get married. I didn't even know how I would pay my car note. At this point, I wasn't certain of anything. I did decide, however, that I was still in love with this man. I wanted nothing more than to marry him and be his wife. I still stayed with him and he even paid my car note. No one had ever done that for me before.

When the month of August arrive, we still hadn't heard a word from the state on the status of his divorce. It was supposed to be a six-month process, which eventually went on for eight months. Then, out of nowhere, the news arrived that his divorce was finally final! I felt like things were starting to look up for us. That dark cloud that was hovering over our heads was finally starting to break. We selected a second special date for the wedding. We came up with Saturday, October 20, 2001.

On the day of our wedding, we were shocked to find out that it was also Sweetest Day. I had never really heard of it. Although it was a day established for love, Sweetest Day is a day that is celebrated on the third Saturday of October. It strongly resembles Valentine's Day. The day was filled with so many emotions and my nerves were out of control.

I was at my mother's house, getting ready to head to the chapel, when Jonathan called me.

"I can't wait to meet you at the altar."

Then, he called me a second time to verify I was showing up. I was so tickled.

"I love you and I'm definitely meeting you at the altar."

As my dad and I came down the aisle, I was so nervous. I'm glad I had my father to keep me together.

We were finally married! My life had begun anew with my husband, even though I wasn't his first wife, like I originally thought. When I became his wife, I had a newfound look on relationships. They definitely weren't anything like the *Lifetime* and *Hallmark* channel romance movies.

In the honeymoon stage of our marriage, things were going well. We had been married for two months and I was still laid off from work. Jonathan came home one day from work and left back out less than an hour later. I really didn't think anything of it at the time. Eventually, he came back home after being gone for two hours. He came in the house quietly.

Then, he said to me, "I have something to talk to you about."

Okay! Here we go again! I thought. The last time he had made that statement, it wasn't good news. He told me the story of what happened at work that day. I thought since he was talking about his job, maybe he was about to tell me that he either got laid off or fired. After he broke the news to me, I wished that was the case.

He ran into an old friend, only for her to tell him that he has a daughter with her sister. At the time, the child was nine years old and the mother never informed him that he was the father of her child. I wasn't as upset with him at first because this child was created way before I came into the picture. It was the aftermath that upset me. The fact that another child was suddenly in the picture and it wasn't with me made me upset. I was now married to a man who not only lied to me about his marital status, but now this man had a second child *that neither one of us knew about*. This was yet another hurdle to get over in our marriage.

He told me, "I'm going to go talk to her mother. I know that I'm going to have to take you with me eventually."

"You goddamn right you are!"

Then, I saw a look of amazement on his face. That's when I realized I must have spoken those words out loud, not in my head. I had cursed at my husband and used the Lord's name in vain before I knew it. I couldn't back down now.

Eventually, we did go to meet his daughter and her mother. We all sat in his car. I was on the passenger side, the mother was behind me, and his daughter sat behind him.

"Now that we are all together, I want to make everything clear. I'm saying this in front of your mother and my wife. If I had known about you, I would have been in your life and your mother never said anything to me about you!"

This man was upset. He took me and my baby in and raised her as his own. I couldn't imagine that he wouldn't do the same for his own. I didn't know how to feel listening to all of this. Part of me was in shock. The other part was angry. How could a woman not at least tell the man he had a child? She had robbed them both of a relationship, without ever giving him a chance. Then he said something that made me speak up.

"I don't need a blood test to prove you are my daughter. The results would be meaningless to me."

That's when I said, "And I'm not accepting this without one!"

We went back and forth. No one was really arguing. We were simply having a little heated discussion. After this so-called meeting was over, we went our separate ways. Even though Jonathan tried throughout the years to spend time with his daughter, he was never able to establish the relationship with her like he had hoped.

As the months went by, I realized that although Jonathan had kept things from me, I was making it *all about me*. I was never taught how to handle things like negative confrontations. I was never taught how to handle heated situations, especially in a marriage. I was quick to judge him and get upset. I wanted to leave the relationship, all because things fell outside the bounds of my expectations based on *Lifetime* and *Hallmark*. This relationship was not what I dreamed it would be. I thought I would have the best marriage ever, with no drama. My marriage would be full of love and romance. All I could do was be upset at myself because I allowed myself to believe that's what relationships were all about: love and romance, hearts and flowers. Instead, I quickly learned that marriages aren't made completely of sugar and spice and everything nice.

In my marriage, I learned that I wasn't *listening*. My mind was already set about how I thought things were supposed to be. Once I started listening, I learned that all marriages go through rough patches. I had to ask myself questions like, "Will I listen to my husband next time he tells me something I don't want to hear, and not be quick to get angry with him? Will I be able to not judge him and not compare him to the fictional husbands from my *Lifetime* and *Hallmark* movies? If I remain in this marriage, will I be able to forgive my husband and be able to live with the fact that he's not perfect?"

As the years went by, and I grew older and wiser; I learned how to be a wife. When Jonathan and I married, I wasn't prepared to be a wife. I didn't know the first thing about it. I was young and I didn't have any adult life experiences. Looking back on those years, I was selfish and spoiled. I was used to getting what I wanted. No one ever told me, "No." I always got my way. I didn't know how to handle major life adjustments.

In the twenty years of us being together, we've grown together. We've been through many hard trials in our marriage, but we have remained supportive for each other. He has been my biggest cheerleader and my biggest investor in my business. He always supports me in all I do.

When things come up in the marriage, I handle them differently. I'm able to listen more and I am quicker to forgive. My husband and I were recently talking about how long he and I have been together. We both agreed that we couldn't believe that we were still together. Our marriage is not perfect. We are still a work in progress. Now I know that marriages require continual work and maintenance. We know that as long as we continue to communicate with each, respond to each other in a positive way, and listen to each other, we'll be just fine. I also pray for him and encourage him daily on anything he wants to accomplish. I thank him for allowing me to share our story. Through all our tests and trials, we have learned to fight for each other by praying for each other and being there for one another.

Marriage Uncut **RELOADED**
Self-Reflection

1. Do your communication skills with your spouse need to improve? Explain.

   _____
   _____
   _____
   _____

2. When you and your spouse have a heavy conversation, are you willing to listen to each other without playing the blame game and getting angry?

   _____
   _____
   _____
   _____

3. Do you and your spouse pray for each other daily? If not, are you willing to start praying for each other and support each other in all that you do?

   _____
   _____
   _____
   _____

About the Author
➥ Angie Green

What many would use as a reason to quit, a reason to give up, Angie Green uses as a reason to trek forward—encouraging others that life after loss can only truly be found in relationship with Christ. Though she's on the other side of some of the worst parts of the journey, she's not oblivious to the fact that this journey is never complete. It's not a race or a sprint. There's no award or medal at the finish line. It's a continual faith walk—many days, hour by hour, minute by minute. And she recognizes that a large part of her hurt and heartache is what helps others heal and find hope. Whether you're looking to inspire a small group of ten, or empower an audience of hundreds, her ability to deliver authentic, motivational messages of hope and healing are sure to catapult attendees to destiny-fulfillment.

Hardwood Floors
by Tenita C. Johnson

UNTOUCHED

Cold, hardwood floors couldn't cover the stench
that's forever ingrained in my nose.

Chilly, freezing almost, I feared asking,
"Can I just put back on my clothes?"

The fact that we had to hide
let me know it was wrong—somewhat;

Fear of what my family would say
made me feel like a hoe, a tramp, a slut.

Many days, I lay awake waiting for the pain,
the shame to subside,

Only to find myself searching for a deeper place to hide.

Grandma always talked about God,
but where in the hell was He?

"Dear God, can you even honor a
prayer from a kid like me?"

Married, children of my own; yet, still locking up.

I've grown. I've matured. But I'm mentally, spiritually, stuck.

You can take a poor black girl out the hood;

Make her put on masks and act like life is all good.

But when depression, suicidal thoughts and bouts of lust become her crutch,

Does the God that she sings about, heard about, have the power to render her untouched?

I was addicted, and I didn't even know it.

The funny thing is that I didn't even realize my form of addiction until I was well into my marriage, which I was singlehandedly tearing up piece by piece. Unlike the good, wholesome Christian girls, I was sexually active with my husband long before we said, "I do!" Even at the young age of fourteen, I wanted sex. But I was *terrified* every time we started. My legs always seemed to lock up before the initial entrance of his penis into my vagina, almost making it impossible for him to penetrate. It always took a few moments for me to get into the mood and groove of it. But once my mind caught up with our bodies, which were midway into the act, I was able to relax and enjoy the ride. As a teenager, my then boyfriend was patient with me when he basically had to pry my legs open for me to relax and "let him in." However, when we married, and I was still locking my legs to the strength of a horse's legs, my husband knew something was seriously wrong.

And it had nothing to do with *him*. It had everything to do with *me*.

I had to be seven years old when I had my first sexual experience. Since my mother had birthed me at fourteen, I stayed with my grandmother most times. Although my mother lived in the same house, my childhood memories of her are faint. Of course, she had to finish and graduate high school, and work. But, when both my grandmother and my mother weren't available to watch me, my older female cousin watched me. Ironically, I always asked to go spend the night over my cousin's house, but my mother and grandmother often refused. I didn't know why back then, but I've come to terms with their reasoning now.

My grandmother had hardwood floors throughout her tiny court way building apartment, where my mother and I, and sometimes my drunk uncle, resided. There was only one bedroom in the apartment, which my grandmother let my mother sleep in. My grandmother's bedroom was actually what should have been the dining room. I'm not sure why or whose idea it was, but I slept in the bed with my grandmother nightly. By the time I was three or four, my grandfather had passed. I have no recollection of him. But, by the way my aunts and uncles talked about him, he wasn't a nice man. Piece by piece, I've picked up that he was abusive in more ways than one to my grandmother and his children. No one in the family will give me the specifics, but as I peel back the layers of history untold, I'm left to imagine the agony and pain my grandmother more than likely endured.

While many people remember waxing hardwood floors on their hands and knees, my memories of the hardwood floors are a tad more gruesome. It was where *she* laid me. Those hardwood floors were where I first experienced oral sex—both giving and receiving. The pain of lying on my back on the floor, and later placing my knees on the floor to return the favor to her, followed me well into adulthood. She didn't necessarily tell me not to tell anyone; it was almost understood.

We always had to do *it* on the *side of the bed* on the floor, instead of on the actual bed.

We always did it when no one else was home.

Many times, we even closed the blinds to make the room darker.

I didn't know it then, but in that exact moment, the root of shame was planted. As a teenager, even though I desired physical sex, I refused oral sex from boys. And I refused to give it to them. I told them I didn't like it. I told them it was nasty and uncomfortable. The truth is that every time someone performed oral sex on me, it reminded me of those *hardwood floors*. So it was safer for me to simply refuse oral sex from anyone even though, many times, I didn't climax from physical sex.

By the time I was fourteen, not only was I addicted to sex, but I was addicted to masturbation and pornography. I found greater pleasure in pleasing myself than engaging in any sexual act with a boy. I can't pinpoint the exact moment I was introduced to pornography; it was almost like it simply *appeared* in my life—and refused to leave. I was in church, but I didn't have enough conviction to stop having sex, watching porn or touching myself. I told myself that I wasn't harming anyone else, and it wasn't a sin if I was engaging sexually with myself.

In those days (sometimes weeks) that I tried to stop having sex, porn and masturbation were my drugs of choice. I was trying to medicate something that was so much deeper than any pill or alcohol bottle could fulfill. I was attempting to satisfy the craving of lust. I was attempting to fill the void of not having a father tell me that I was worth the wait. I was rocking myself to sleep spiritually, emotionally and physically—often masturbating two or three times a day when no one was home, only to fall into a deep sleep.

I told myself that I *needed* it. I needed to feel like I'd felt the first time I actually started to *enjoy* the oral sex my cousin performed on me. I needed to feel the release. I needed to feel in control of pleasing myself when no one else around me felt like I was worth it. I equated the sex, the porn, the masturbation to love. The reality is I was chasing what I now know as the spirit of lust, which was masked as *love*.

In college, I found myself sleeping with too many men to count, many of them whose names I can't remember. From one-night stands when we left the club drunk, to "hidden" relationships with college fraternity men—who invited me over once the sun went down, but acted like they didn't know me when they saw me at the student center. Even in college, I was against receiving oral sex. I told myself I didn't need it. I could please myself much faster and easier. But with a little alcohol in my system, I gained enough courage to perform oral sex on men—something I vowed I would never do. By the end of freshman year of college, I had contracted chlamydia—*for the second time.* When my mother found out I was sexually active at fourteen, just as she had been, she took me to the doctor for testing. I tested positive then for chlamydia and brushed it off. Because there is a cure, a series of pills, I didn't take it as serious as AIDS or HIV. I knew I was going to live. So, I continued to live haphazardly in college.

When I later caught up with the man who is now my husband at the age of twenty, he was shocked that I even offered to perform oral sex on him. Again, we'd been sexually active with each other since I was fourteen years old. He wasn't used to the twenty-year-old Tenita. But, he didn't refuse, either. Once again, he tried to perform oral sex on me and I refused. All I could think about was those *hardwood floors*. I told him I simply didn't desire it. I didn't need it. It was as if I had watched so much porn, and pleased myself so much, that no one else could please me sexually. If it didn't look, sound or feel like sex did in porn, it wasn't real to me. It wasn't good enough.

At the time, I didn't know about human trafficking. I didn't know that many of the women in pornography are under the influence of drugs, or they are forced to perform sexual acts in front of the camera against their will—and actually act like they are enjoying themselves! I didn't know that masturbation was a sin. I thought as long as I wasn't hurting another human being, and I wasn't in fornication, that I was living a righteous life. As I matured in Christ, God began to ask me thought-provoking rhetorical questions. He already knew the answers. But He had to ask me in a certain way to get me to see sin the way He sees sin.

God asked me, "Would you masturbate in front of your children or your husband? Would you watch porn if your husband was lying next to you? Why do you think you masturbate multiple times a day, and you can never seem to get enough?"

I hung my head in shame and awe, already knowing the answers to the questions, unfortunately. That's when God revealed to me how to know the difference between light and darkness. There is no in between. He reminded me that, every time I prepared to masturbate,

I closed the blinds or drapes to darken the room. When I had sex with men, I always needed to have sex under the covers or sheets. I didn't like a man looking at me naked in the light—or even without the sheets covering my body for that matter. I didn't even like having sex in the morning time. My drive was (and still is) at its highest at night. The truth of the whole matter was that I would never masturbate or watch porn in the room with my children or my husband because of the level of *shame* I'd developed over time. Shame had taken root at the age of seven and refused to let me go. I would stop during fasts or during weeks where I was extremely busy. But as soon as I had idle time, the thought to masturbate or watch porn reared its ugly head once again.

When I married my husband, he said something to me that, at first, offended me. The truth usually does, though.

He said, "You equate sex to love. And if we're not having sex, you feel like I don't love you."

I was ashamed of that truth, but he had hit the nail on the head, allowing it to pierce the very depths of my soul. In that moment, I was confronted with the ugly truth that many attempt to sweep under a rug—leaving them shackled to shame, fear, guilt and low self-esteem. When my husband was angry with me, and we didn't have sex for days or weeks at a time, I thought he was going to leave me. He threatened to leave me many times before, so it was only a matter of time before he actually left and didn't come back. So, I thought. He was going to leave me, just like my mother and grandmother had left me with my older cousin, who introduced me to oral sex. He was going to leave me like my father had left me—destitute and broken without a clear definition of my identity. He was going to leave me, alone and depressed.

To my surprise, no matter how many times he threatened to leave, through every storm, he chose to stay. Even after my infidelity when our marriage was in shambles, he chose to love me through it. He chose to pray me through it. He chose to cover me in prayer and speak well over me. He supported me by paying for six years of *individual* counseling, which totally transformed my mind and, hence, our marriage. Many people get into a marriage and think that they need years of marital counseling. The truth is most people need some form of individual counseling before they attempt to join in holy matrimony to anyone. I didn't know who I was in Christ when I married. I didn't like myself. I battled suicidal thoughts and bouts of depression too many times to count. And, unlike many people think, my addiction to masturbation and pornography didn't cease when I got married. If anything, it increased.

When my husband was mad at me, or tired from work, I defaulted to pleasing myself. It was quicker and I didn't have to deal with him rejecting me. I didn't know I was building taller, invisible walls that he would later have to tear down every time we tried to be intimate. I didn't realize the spirit of division and lust that I was allowing to operate in my marriage. As long as I didn't step outside the marriage with another man, I didn't consider it as cheating on my husband. It took the wisdom of one pastor to open my eyes to the damage I was causing unintentionally.

He said to me, "When you masturbate, or watch porn and please yourself, you are operating in a form of prostitution."

I wasn't a prostitute! I'd never worked a street corner a day in my life. The raw truth will first offend you, then it will change you. In the Word of God, 1 Corinthians 6:19-20 (NIV) says, *Do you not know that your bodies are temples of the Holy Spirit, who is in you, whom you have received from God? You are not your own; you were bought at a price. Therefore honor God with your bodies.* Prostitutes don't honor God with their bodies. They use their bodies to earn money, which has become their god. And, I'm sad to say, I was no better than them.

As I matured in my walk with Christ, I realized if I was going to truly break this stronghold, I had to be intentional about my time. I had to be intentional about what I allowed to enter my ear gates and eye gates. I immediately asked my husband to cancel the subscription to premium channels on cable. I threw out all of my pornographic DVDs in large, black trash bags. That's how many I had acquired since college. I started being strategic about what I watched on TV. I can't watch sex scenes, or even some kissing scenes, in a movie or a TV show. I immediately get aroused. I know I can't listen to certain music, either. Although I love Brian McKnight, if I listen to him, I immediately fall into a sensual, sexual mood. There are even certain songs or albums that remind me of old flings from college that I simply know I can't listen to. I also gave certain friends permission to hold me accountable to my healing and deliverance journey. My friends would call or text me and ask if I had watched porn or masturbated recently. They prayed with me over the phone or in person too many times to count. This is a stronghold that requires accountability, prayer, counseling and more to break. Its roots run deep.

I'd be lying if I told you the thoughts don't come anymore. More times than not, those thoughts come when no one is home and I'm sleepy or sluggish. They come when I lie down at night and my husband may not be in bed yet. Of course, if I watch a show or a movie, or listen to a certain type of music, my desires are heightened. But I know firsthand the damage masturbation and porn has caused to me as an individual, a wife and a mother. My husband and I are strategic about making sure these strongholds don't get passed on in our bloodline to our children or their children. We don't want our children to ever experience molestation. We don't want our children to have to work through pulling up the roots of strongholds like masturbation and addiction to pornography. We want our children to live wholesome lives as individuals and spouses once they marry and have children of their own. Life in general has enough trouble of its own. We don't want our children to carry any extra baggage into their next journey of life.

It took me years to learn it, but now I understand that masturbation and addiction to pornography is another form of slavery. Mentally, I was bound and shackled. I needed my "fix" every day, multiple times a day. The enemy wanted to keep me "high" and strung out on drugs that society doesn't know how to rehabilitate. There was no five-step program or detox program that would allow me to go cold turkey. I had to walk out the journey of healing and deliverance day by day, hour by hour, minute by minute, as the Holy Spirit revealed the underlying roots and effects that kept me stuck wanting more. God was patient enough with me to reveal those things I was mature enough to handle as I walked through the journey. He didn't dump it all on me at once. He lovingly slowly, but surely, transformed my mind and allowed me to see those things as He sees them.

Many times, we make excuses for our sin. We say, "God knows my heart." We take God's grace and mercy for granted. We focus on God's love, but not His correction. The Word of God is clear. Whom He loves, He chastises, just as we do our own children. For years, I told myself that I needed to masturbate or watch porn to go to sleep. I needed it to fulfill my lustful desires so I wouldn't have sex with anyone. I needed it to make myself feel good, to make myself feel worthy of love. However, one thing is for certain: light and darkness cannot coexist. As soon as light shows up in a room, darkness ceases. God is that light. When He showed up in my life, and truly began to walk me through total transformation, any sign of darkness had to cease.

I had to forgive my cousin. After all, someone had to be touching her inappropriately in order for her to perform oral sex on me in her youth. Where does a child get that from? It had to be deposited into her in order for her to perform the act. I had to forgive my mother and grandmother for leaving me vulnerable. I had to forgive them for not protecting me enough to not let this happen over and over again. I had to forgive them for keeping so many family secrets that it kept not only them bound, but me as well. I now realize that I'm not just working through my individual strongholds. I'm yet working to uproot those things that were passed on to me from generations of people who chose to suffer in silence. I'm yet working to uproot the family curses that continue to try to ride on the bloodline. My husband and I are strategic and intentional about telling our children what we have been through and overcame—so that they don't have to fight the same battles. We work to heal marriages and families across the nation, allowing them to break generational curses off their family bloodline and rewrite their family history.

There's so much in my life that remains a mystery. I'm certain that as I grow in my relationship with Christ, He will reveal that which I am able to accept and process healthily.

People say, "What you don't know can't hurt you."

I beg to differ. It's those things that *I didn't know* that affected my life the most, unfortunately.

Be committed to your individual healing, and your marriage will be healed. The transformation you want to see in your marriage starts with *you*.

Marriage Uncut **RELOADED**
SELF-REFLECTION

1. What individual strongholds do you need to work through to get total healing and deliverance?

   _____

   _____

2. Who do you need to forgive in order for you to be totally free?

   _____

   _____

3. What happened to you as a child that has negatively affected your marriage?

   _____

   _____

4. What is God's purpose for your marriage?

   _____

   _____

5. What has God revealed to you about *you* that you need to come to grips with?

   _____

   _____

About the Author
➥ Tenita C. Johnson

From losing a set of twins the day after she and her husband were married, to years of unemployment, suicidal thoughts and blended family woes, she soon learned that the only way out of every fire is to go through it. After going through the fire numerous times, and coming out unscathed, she realized that every fire was orchestrated by God to burn some things off of her to make her better. Not only that, every fire gave her a greater testimony to share with others who may be encountering the same things.

Through her books, Tenita encourages readers nationwide to know that with every test comes a predetermined victory. The young girl who once thought she wasn't good enough has blossomed into a woman of faith who knows that, with God, she is more than just enough. She makes a deliberate choice to live her best life now and walk in her God-given purpose daily, and encourages others to do the same.

For more information, visit www.soitiswritten.net.

A Little Drama Goes a Long Way
by Orlando Crawford

I was only 17, and I was about to be a father.

We'd met two years prior and fell in love rapidly. We began dating and she seemed to be the perfect one for me. We married at the age of 18. It seemed like the right thing to do, seeing as though I had got her pregnant. I wanted to do the *Christian thing*, so I married her. One afternoon in the middle of the week, we went to Toledo. However, we couldn't get married because I didn't have my original birth certificate. They gave us quite a hard time, but then we ran into a pastor who had the "hook up" in another county. We followed him and got married. The issue with us trying to get married in Toledo should have been a sign, but I ignored it. All I could see was my future with her.

Since we were married and had a baby at a young age, I worked two or three jobs to maintain the family's needs. Two years after our first child was born, we had twins. *Twins!* And I was only 20 years old. Soon after the twins, my wife was diagnosed with postpartum depression. She became homesick. However, she refused to get help. We didn't know how to cope with postpartum depression. It seemed like many women experienced it, and it was just a part of having a baby. We later found out that not every woman experiences this, nor does every woman recover from it.

She became suicidal, aggressive and temperamental. This caused her to relapse, which brought about images and experiences from her childhood trauma. This drove her back to the abuse she experienced as a child. So much so that she invited the very individual who abused her to move in with us. One day after coming home from work, I was met with my mother-in-law and sister-in-law having moved into our home. She had not asked me if they could move in at all. Immediately, I had two additional people in my household to take care of. This was the beginning of a downward spiral. Hell was the name of this journey. My wife did things that were *initially* uncharacteristic of her, which unfolded a multitude of circumstances that I could have never imagined.

After the birth of our twins, when I arrived home, I had a letter from the Family Independence Agency. This letter said that my wife had committed fraud. It questioned whether or not she was my wife because she did not carry my last name. (I later found out that she never legally changed her name because she had intended to commit fraud all along.) Now, I had to appear in court. While in court, the judge informed me that she had committed fraud using other people's addresses to get benefits, even though she was married. I was not listed on her benefits and, because of that, they charged me as her husband to pay back the fraud she had committed. I also had to pay for the labor and delivery costs of our children. Under the law, I claimed innocent spouse, but the courts told me that it did not apply to this situation. So, I had to pay $146,000 over the next ten years. This wasn't my debt! This wasn't my fault nor was it my mishap! I had to pay over $140,000 for someone who clearly didn't think about me, her children, her future or the consequences.

Soon after the postpartum depression episodes came the family feuds. I was feuding against her family because she kept moving them into the house, and I kept kicking them out. As time progressed, the fights grew more aggressive. Soon, I found out that she was abusing prescription medication. She also began to live promiscuously outside the marriage. She once told me that she felt like her childhood was taken away from her, and she blamed me for that. Her abuse, neglect and childhood suffocation happened many years before I met her; however, I can understand her feeling like a bit of her youth was taken since I made her a mother at such an early age. While my support may have helped her adjust to this new life of being a wife and a mother, eventually, it caused her to change. I believe she grew to resent our marriage. Over the course of our young marriage, she committed adultery, become pregnant by another man, had abortions, contracted sexually transmitted diseases, abused prescription and recreational drugs, and was sexually active with both men and women. After all of that, in my mind, I could no longer stay married to her.

But, because of my love for her, and my desire for my marriage to work, I was willing to do whatever it took. I suggested counseling. She refused. Then came the final straw. After a great deal of time had passed, and we had not been sexually active, she told me that she was pregnant and she wanted an abortion.

I yelled, "Get in the car now!"

We drove to my doctor's office for a pregnancy test. If she was, it was not mine and I was pissed. We confirmed that she was indeed pregnant. While we were at the office, they also ran tests for all sexually transmitted diseases. She tested positive. I was tested as well, but I came up negative. Clearly, my wife had been cheating on me for quite some time, and she didn't have sense enough to protect herself. Even though we had been through so much in prior years, nothing could have hurt me more than to sit in the doctor's office with those results in front of me. She didn't apologize. She didn't acknowledge her wrong. Furthermore, she had the nerve to be mad at me because I took her to the doctor!

Days later, I called a friend of mine who owned an apartment building and asked him for a favor. That same day, I got the keys and moved my soon to be ex-wife into an apartment with our children and everything she needed to function. I wanted to keep my children with me, but she fought me on it. The police just told me to take it to court. I no longer wanted to be married to her.

Right after she moved out, I filed for the divorce. The divorce proceedings took a year. But once it was all over, I had a party. I was drunk as a skunk (and I'm not a big drinker). The drinking that night was just a mask to cover all my pain, but it was a celebration, too. I was legally free from her and she could no longer pin her criminal activities to me.

Six months after the divorce, I started dating because I thought I was ready. After a couple of months of dating, my ex-wife heard through our children and nosy neighbors that it was getting serious with someone. We started dating more regularly, including overnight visits. One morning at 3 a.m., we were awakened by loud tires screeching outside, followed by a banging on the door. It was my ex-wife.

She was screaming, "I'm going to kill you and that bitch!"

I ran downstairs to address her screaming and banging, but I knew I needed to call the police. As I was talking to her through the door, with superhero strength, she barreled through the door, with my daughter and her niece behind her. My ex-wife started destroying my house. She appeared to be under the influence of a controlled substance or alcohol. I restrained her, picked her up, and put her out the house. By this time, the house was destroyed. She pulled down all the plates out of my cupboard, screaming, "I bought these plates and no other bitch is gonna eat off these mother@#$%^ plates!"

She punched me as I tried to pull her out the house. She tripped and fell on some dumbbells and told everyone later that I had broken her ribs. She ran out to the truck, which I had bought her, and backed up over my car, resulting in $5,000 worth of damage. The harassment didn't stop there. Shortly following that event, we discussed the child support she had not received yet. I informed her that the money did in fact come out of my check.

"You should get it soon," I told her.

That next morning after arriving to work, one of my coworkers screamed, "Orlando, look out!" I immediately turned around and was staring right at my ex-wife's truck speeding towards me. I jumped out of the way, diving between two cars. She was trying to kill me! *Literally!* She had our oldest daughter in the front seat.

I could hear my daughter crying and screaming, "Stop, Mommy! What are you doing?!"

She rolled down the passenger window, spit in my face and screamed, "I hate you!"

Then, she drove off. It was like a scene from a movie. This all happened just before my workday started, so all of my coworkers were outside since I worked the afternoon shift. After that incident, one of my female coworkers told me she had lost her mind after having those children. At the time, we had four children, including a set of twins. Her irrational behavior may have been linked to postpartum depression, but she also abused recreational drugs and prescription drugs. The combination created a whirlwind.

I kept my distance from her, and even between started drinking profusely. I drank daily. While I got drunk every day, I had so many thoughts. But the ones that stood out in particular were the thoughts that told me that I could not love like this, and that this was surely going to kill me. I stopped drinking, went cold turkey and examined myself. I started going to church and I studied the Word more. I was raised in the church and I knew that God was my source. I was seeking to find Him even more during this time. I came to understand that you cannot make anyone love you. God also taught me how to love myself. He restored my soul. During the restoration process, I still had more hurdles dealing with my ex-wife and trying to see my children.

More pain followed: the pain of not seeing my children. She wouldn't allow me to see them and the courts were on her side. For the first year and a half, I was able to have my children with me every weekend. We had such a great time, whether we ate hot dogs and drank pop, or went to an arcade and ate a Hot 'n' Ready. We just loved being together. I could see their pain and I prayed for them constantly. I told them that I loved them, no matter how far apart we were. After a year and a half, I started dating again. That's when my access to my children ceased. I fought years to get custody of them, or even to just visit them. But she kept moving so I couldn't locate her. She did not disclose her address to the state, so they had difficulty finding her too. I was missing out on my children's' lives and she didn't care.

Through this marriage, I have two boys and two girls. They were so impressionable at the time and definitely didn't understand. How could they? I periodically saw my children at family gatherings throughout the years, but it was brought to my attention that their mother was telling them that I didn't want to see them, which caused them to *want* to stay away from me. I wasn't even invited to my oldest daughter's graduation. This hurt me so badly. This was not what I intended. I loved my wife and I wanted my marriage to work. But, I could not fight her demons, her past, her hurt and her drug addiction. But, I was more than willing to help her wholeheartedly. Though the marriage brought about so much pain, the most joyous events were the birth of my children. They were and are the biggest blessings in my life.

After this season of my life, I felt like I had built a box, a wall of protection. I thought I was over the marriage, but I hadn't healed because I hardened my heart. This is why the counseling was so important. This marriage caused me to not trust others, especially women. So, this is why I encourage anyone who is engaged or married, and the relationship feels even remotely unhealthy, or you are questioning something, get to counseling and talk about it. Make sure the fullness of the issue is discussed in patience, with compassion and honesty. When talking to your spouse, be sure to display the same level of love and respect you desire. And *listen!* I mean actually *listen*. What are you in the relationship or marriage for if not to spend the rest of your life with someone you want? Your desire should be to meet every need for your spouse and to keep them happy.

If you find that one spouse or partner does not desire, nor want the counseling, that may be a clear sign that struggle is in your future. Never allow your pain to cause pain to someone else. Never try to get revenge because you are hurting. You will just hurt others. If you are in this place, find your peace. It took me several years and much counseling to stay sane. I still had to pay this $146,000 back and I wasn't even cordially speaking to my ex-wife. I spent over 20 years paying the debt and state garnishments. I felt hopeless.

It is very hard to find healing by yourself. You have to be honest and take the first step to heal. Stay away from the opinions of others who have no good fruit (those who have a history of disastrous relationships or those who have never been married). Seek God for guidance. It is my hope, though this portion of my life story had disappointment, betrayal and pain, that you are also able to see that I made it through it all. It may sound like a cliché, but it was truly by the grace of God that I did not commit suicide. It crossed my mind several times during those years of not being able to see my children. It is from these lessons that I have learned a great deal of what to do and what *not* to do. I am a man that reverences the Word of God. I sought wise counsel after my bouts of depression from the divorce and the separation from my children. I was determined to move forward.

I became a man of affirmations. For me, writing down positive affirmations helped to encourage me daily. I knew that one day, the depression, suicidal thoughts, pain, rejection and hurt from this marriage would come to an end. Those affirmations changed my life. I stood in front of the mirror and spoke to myself, "I am healed! I am wealthy! I am healthy! I am blessed! I am loved! I am not forgotten! I am worthy of love! I am trusted!" –These positive affirmations pushed me through to be able to share this with you. The more I spoke the affirmations, the stronger I became. Hope began to grow within me, and I pray that it does the same for you.

Choose wisely. Don't be afraid to love and show love. Love the person who shows you love and the one who gives love back to you. Believe what people show and tell you. Don't try to dismiss a red flag. If it shows up, speak to it and discuss it! If you've found that you have a history of toxic or destructive relationships, get help before moving into your next one. Be honest with yourself. It will save you a lot of pain. Get counseling. It is okay to pray, read self-help books, and seek wise friendships or advice. But, I strongly suggest counseling after enduring a hurtful relationship.

If you are in a toxic marriage (Orlando's definition - a marriage where verbal, financial, physical, sexual or mental abuse is occurring and you have such a stronghold with them that you can't seem to let go of, even though you know they are not good for you), get help now. Have those lengthy, thorough and honest conversations about everything from your favorite fruit to how many people you have slept with. Ask questions like the following: Do you battle with depression? If so, did you get help? How is your credit? Have you ever been addicted to drugs? Have you ever been arrested? Do you like your parents? How was your childhood? Were you ever molested or abused? Answering these questions will save your life! That marriage was hell and I learned more than my lesson.

Or had I?

Marriage Uncut RELOADED
SELF-REFLECTION

1. What are the red flags in your relationships that you noticed but ignored?

   _____

   _____

2. What do you do when your hope in love is crushed?

   _____

   _____

3. How will you find the help you need to heal?

   _____

   _____

4. Will you allow your hurt to cripple you or propel you?

   _____

   _____

5. What are some of the things you are going to do to make your marriage successful?

   _____

   _____

About the Author
➥ Orlando Crawford

Orlando Crawford had a childhood surrounded by family, friends and church. Ideally, Orlando had the seemingly perfect childhood. However, for him, it lacked something he desperately needed: love and attention. Orlando sought to find love in any way he could. While he found it, it came with a price. Through a damaging, destructive marriage, Orlando has been able to take his turmoil and turn it into triumph. Orlando has five beautiful children and now has a healthy, fulfilling marriage. He has a story to tell and his hope is that you learn, but live your life to the fullest. He has a passion to invoke men to fulfill their God-given destiny, despite a history of poor decisions. Orlando teaches others how not to allow the pain of bad relationships to hinder the great call God for His people to lead, love and prosper.

Wrong Turn Down Relationship Road
by Natasha Crawford

Submit? Yeah, right. I refused to *submit*. I hated the very word itself.

Long before I had met my ex-husband, I had made up my mind that I was not going to, nor was I willing to, submit to any man. He was no exception.

My mother always told me, "Tasha, all men are dogs!" This is what I heard consistently throughout my teenage and young adult years, and I had no reason to believe otherwise. So, that phrase was planted in the back of mind, even in the times I tried to forget it. But, in so many instances during my dating of various men, that was the consensus. They *were* "all dogs."

I had my first sexual experience at the age of 16 with an eighteen-year-old. He was supposed to graduate high school, but he dropped out and was living in his mom's basement. He didn't have a job or a car. He had no direction for his life and no ambition. I still can't believe I gave up one of my most precious possessions to *that* individual. I didn't love him, but he had experienced sex already and was far more *advanced* in that area, which intrigued me. Love had nothing to do with it. He was different than the typical suburban boys I was surrounded by, so I took a leap—a not so great leap.

My mother couldn't stand him and she was very vocal about it, too. But it didn't stop me from seeing him. I was full of rebellion and lust. However, to her delight, we didn't stay together long because I found out that he stole his sister's bracelet to give to me as a Christmas gift. I was *done*. So, I can honestly say that, from the beginning of my teenage years, I made very poor decisions when it came to the opposite sex. As years progressed, the decisions held a bit more depth. I began to *love* more so than *like* men. Yet, it was still a clear example of me not knowing my worth. When you battle with low self-esteem, and do not recognize your value, you settle—in all areas of your life. Many men can see a woman's worth and can tell if she knows it or not. Unfortunately, many may take advantage of that woman.

Many people say that the reason women pick certain men is because they exhibit characteristics of their fathers or who they wished their father would have been. I agree. My father was distant emotionally. Many call it being "old school" in the way that men of a certain era expressed love—or the lack thereof. He was a provider. He paid the bills, kept the grass cut, and watched the news every night. He was not one to express much emotion, nor show genuine love toward his family. I only remember hearing, "I love you, my daughter," after a glass of bourbon or whiskey. The smell of a pipe also filled the room at the time. It was an uneasy feeling, and it wasn't comforting at all. Those words came from a place of intoxication and they did nothing for me. Hence, I chased the same type of men in all of my relationships. They were all distant. They lacked intimacy. They were emotionally unavailable often. My ex-husband fit that category—*mostly*. He was clearly not the man for me. So much pain, disappointment, hurt and abuse followed the, "I do!" He was hell to live with, and it was only a matter of time before it ended.

I had all the red flags. In the dating phase, he was flirting with every attractive woman we encountered. He told me I was insecure because when he flirted with women, I always checked him. He told me I was being non-submissive, even before we married, because I didn't agree with him on certain issues. I knew he wasn't the one, but lust and enough love led me to marry him. One time, he received counsel from a minister at our church. In that counsel, the minister told him that as I became his wife, and even during our dating phase, that I should always place him before my child. Well, I disagreed with that wholeheartedly.

My thought process was, "Dude, you're new to the game and my son is my son! I'm still in trial-and-error mode with you, so I'm not putting you before my son!" Because I disagreed with him on that, he said that I was not a submissive woman. He was concerned that I would not be a submissive wife and he was very disturbed that I would not put him before my son. Well, we eventually "got over it" because we just didn't talk about it anymore. It was like an unspoken understanding, but it left a big question mark for the both of us.

This is a challenge that a lot of single women find themselves in. They struggle with inviting or allowing a man into their life with their children, then totally submitting to that man without him submitting to God. I understand the single life because I've been there and done that. It has so many challenges, but adding a man to the mix causes even more challenges. Ladies, you have to be very careful about the man that you choose to come into your life when you have children. We see it on the news so often, and it is so unfortunate. But when you make poor choices, it can cost you your life and the lives of others. In some instances, it may not cost you your life physically, but it can cost you mentally, emotionally, verbally, spiritually and naturally.

When you are not mentally and emotionally ready for a fulfilling and complete relationship, you can turn it into a whirlwind.

I've learned to give myself time to heal from a bad relationship or break-up, and that time is different for everyone. Don't let anyone rush you! But, when you rush into things, and your mental and emotional state is still unhealthy and broken, you will attract unhealthy and broken men. Yes, you could come together and heal together. But, are you really willing to take that risk if God hasn't led you to do so? There's too much at risk when you're a single mother to invite just any man into your life haphazardly. My desire is for every woman to make a sound, healthy decision before getting into any relationship. Walking into my previous marriage, I thought that I was whole. However, I found that as we continued to date and into the marriage that I was far from whole.

In my marriage, I suffered emotionally, verbally and mentally—but never physically. I've been told that verbal and mental abuse is much more damaging than physical, and I don't have anything to compare it to. However, I can definitely tell you that I would never again want to experience either one. Never be anyone's punching bag! When you have found that one who you believe God has sent you, enjoy the dating phase. Talk about everything and really get to know one another. Pay attention to every detail, no matter how small.

There was a time during our initial dating phase when I called it quits. It was about nine months into the dating phase. I felt like I had a clear answer on whether or not he was the one for me. I told him with confidence that I could no longer see him.

He asked me, "Well, can I come over to get a few of my things?"

I agreed. *Why did I do that?* He came over and told me that he believed I was the one. He started crying. After that, I stood strong for a couple of days, then I made the phone call, asking if I could stop by. When I got there, he was cooking fried chicken. He stood pretty arrogantly and confidently because he knew why I had stopped by. I changed my mind. I had decided that I may have been wrong in my decision to stop dating him. He accepted my 'return' and we moved forward. We continued to date, but we both had reservations for different reasons. We couldn't stop having sex. It was like a drug.

One day he said to me, "I might as well marry you because we can't seem to stop having sex, and I want to be with you." It was genuine, but not the right decision. Well, even though I knew that wasn't a good enough reason, we went with it because I felt like I loved him, too. I thought this could work. But, to my disappointment, I made yet another wrong turn down "relationship road."

Life has enough challenges as it is. But to marry the wrong man made it even worse. But, it wasn't his fault. It was *mine*. I saw the signs, sensed the need for caution, but went ahead and married him anyway because I loved him. Right? Wrong. It was much deeper than that. I loved the thought of a man with good credit. I loved the thought of a man who was good at saving his money. I loved the thought of frequent sex, too! Jackpot!

After we said, "I do," the marriage was pretty much done. It sounds cliché-ish, but it was the beginning of the end. We met in the summer and we didn't go out much. He always cooked since he was a good cook. We also attended the same church. So, after church (almost every Sunday), we stopped by the grocery store to grab food for dinner. I noticed that he had a bad habit of flirting. One day when we stopped at the grocery store, we were walking to the car and he saw a female acquaintance. When they glanced at each other, she smirked.

She said, "Hey!"

He said, "Hey, Shorty. You good?" I looked at her. I looked at him.

She smirked and said, "Yeah, I'm good."

Now, to me, that whole scenario was disrespectful. One, he didn't remotely acknowledge me (his girlfriend at the time). Then, the way that they looked at each other with a little smirk bothered me. But obviously, it didn't bother me enough. I continued to date him, even though that flirting disturbed me. Clearly, I made a choice to ignore that red flag.

Ladies, if something disturbs you about someone you're dating, it would behoove you not to ignore it. I know we have the tendency to sweep things under the rug or hope that things will change as he sees how amazing we are. But I've come to find in my life's experiences that just does not happen. You cannot be so desperate that you just accept any man that compliments you, rubs you the right way or buys you flowers. You have to dig deeper. You have to look at the character of that man. Cooking your dinner and buying you flowers doesn't mean he's a good guy. That just means that he is possibly a good cook and he is great at picking out flowers. That doesn't constitute the right boyfriend or husband for you.

If it walks like a duck and quacks like a duck, it's a duck! So, after seeing so many red flags, you then have to make a decision whether or not you want to marry this duck. Remember that settling comes with consequences. For me, I saw those changes quickly in my household and it was unsettling, to say the least.

Instantly, he made changes to our daily structure. He created strict chores and responsibilities for my nine-year-old son. Because of those rules, we had limited interaction with family and friends. My family did not care for him, and he felt the same toward them. The sex dissipated, too. I became uninterested. Due to our more frequent arguing, and lack of communication, the sex dwindled drastically. I never desired it from him. To be really honest, I believe he only came to me for sex because I was legally and spiritually his wife. He was still trying to be "honorable" to some extent. This marriage took on a totally different path than what I imagined when I planned for my life after the altar. It went far left and eventually had to come full circle. We had to make a decision.

In the beginning, some changes were needed. But we had to make changes in moderation because his approach caused immediate rebellion and disdain. I started considering divorce because of our fighting and complaining. I was simply tired of it. I noticed that my husband would say things to put my son down. One time, we were at my son's school and my son was stuffing his homework into his drawer. When I discussed it with my then-husband, he said, "Well, I'm glad it happened because you think he's so perfect. You needed to see that he has faults, too."

I told him, "I don't feel like my son is perfect, but he is a good boy. He may not make the best decisions all the time, but no, he's not perfect."

We'd continue arguing and yelling back and forth because he was adamant about me seeing my son's faults. Though this disturbed me, I didn't let it end the marriage. There was clearly some resentment and jealousy brewing, though. There were some underlying issues that caused him to even bring something like this up. When he purposely pointed out my son's negative traits, I knew that there was more to uncover.

As the years went on, he continued to make sly and demeaning comments about my son on various occasions. One time at church, one of the deacons in the church complimented and commended my son for the way he speaks, his maturity and his respectful nature.

Immediately, my husband said, "Yeah, you may think he's respectful. But ask him how many times I have to tell him to clean his room."

Why did he feel the need to discount the compliments with a negative remark about my son? This continued throughout the entire course of our marriage, but I did not realize how damaging his words and actions toward my son were. I found out years later after our divorce that he had threatened him a few times in various situations. I believe that, had I known about these threats to my son, I would have left him a long time ago. It was one thing to argue with me, demean me and belittle me. But to purposely attack my son verbally, emotionally and mentally was inexcusable. Unfortunately, women accept and deal with much more than we should. Many times, we don't realize how staying in a damaging relationship damages everyone else associated with that relationship.

From the time I started dating my then-husband, my best friend did not care for his character and he did not care for her. To him, being married meant that I was totally submissive to him. That was a challenge for me because I did not feel that I should submit to a man who didn't seem to submit to God, nor to our union. Just because we were married to one another didn't mean that we were submitted to the union. My best friend and I experienced years of separation because she did not get along with my husband over the course of my seven years of living in the house with him. We separated when I was seven months pregnant with our youngest son. I only saw my best friend about a dozen times in that time frame, and that hurt. I felt torn. As unhappy as I was in the marriage, I chose not to add more arguing and discord to the union. So, I talked to my best friend when he wasn't around. We emailed each other more often than we saw each other to keep in touch. But there was still a disconnect between us. I'm sure it hurt her as much as it hurt me. She respected that I made a choice to marry and love him, but I'm sure it hurt her because that choice caused us to be disconnected. However, it didn't change the true friendship and love we have for one another.

Again, when you make decisions to be in relationships that are hurtful, damaging and abusive, you cause heartache for not just yourself and your spouse—but literally everyone connected to you. Sometimes, you don't realize the suffering until years later. At that time, it may be repairable, or it may take another 10 years to heal and rebuild the relationship.

Premarital and marital counseling is essential. I encourage every married, or soon-to-be married person to seek counseling. Counseling is a tool to help the couple talk about issues that maybe they never really thought about. It helps to bring out those things that maybe the couple didn't know were there. When you're talking about marrying someone, you are marrying the entire person. That means you are marrying the person with their childhood issues, their daddy issues, their gambling problem, the pornography issues and more!

I found out a lot about myself during and after my first marriage. It was quite alarming, yet hopeful. I had not realized how much my lack of confidence and low self-esteem had played such a large role in my relationships. From experience, my advice is to get yourself right first before you enter into the next relationship. Keep your mind clear so you can hear what God is saying. He will not direct you into a troubling relationship. That marriage was verbally, emotionally, mentally and financially abusive. I was controlled by what he wanted and what he told me to do. I wasn't good at managing my money. He controlled all the finances; I could not spend a dollar. There were quite a few instances throughout the course of our marriage when I wanted to hang out with my friends or go visit my brother, who was just a few cities away, and I couldn't go because he wouldn't give me gas money.

He would tell me, "If you go, don't ask me for any gas money!" Out of my fear of not being able to manage money, and knowing that he would not give me a dime, I oftentimes didn't go. As a matter of fact, I very rarely attended any social events unless it was something that he and I were attending together. The great part about that was that I loved his family. I still do! They are a bunch of great men and women, and I had so much fun being around them. That's another one of the downfalls to a marriage that ends up in divorce. Sometimes, it separates you from your ex's family, even though you didn't have a problem with their family! Even now, when I see or communicate with his family on social media, it is always great to connect with them to see how they're doing. It's good to know that the connection we had was genuine.

I don't believe many of our family members were clearly aware of what was going on in our household. If they had a judgment or an assumption, they never shared it with me. My family occasionally asked me, "Is everything okay? How are the boys?" They kept it simple. It was rare that I saw my brother, so he didn't question me heavily. He didn't want to cause any friction or cause me to distance myself even more. I had never heard of financial abuse until after my divorce, but I realized that I actually experienced some of that.

One time, we discussed finances and he asked me not to spend a dime on anything. I agreed. Well, one day, I stopped at the gas station and purchased gas and a bag of chips. The gas was acceptable, but the chips were not in his eyes. Because he had asked me not to spend a dime, we argued and he did not speak to me for three days. *Literally, because of a dollar!* It just seemed way over the top to be so upset about a dollar. He says it was the principle of the matter and my refusal to be submissive. I say it was B.S.! It was just another form of control.

In hindsight, I can see that there were clear signs to, "Abort! Abort!" But I stayed. I stayed in hope that there would be a change *in him*. I knew *I* needed to change a few things. But of course I made his changes much more prevalent and necessary. One should not ignore their need for change and the obvious signs of a toxic relationship. You cannot ignore the obvious red flags in your relationship. You may need to slow down until you investigate further.

What was it about me that looked past his flirting? What was it about me that allowed sex to happen, even when spiritually, I felt I needed to wait? What was it about me that allowed him a level of control that was so slight that I ignored it? It was low self-esteem and fear.

I took time to discover when, why and where. To be honest, I am still learning, healing and gaining a better understanding as I move forward. But, I have been blessed to get past the pain of a divorce, after suffering silently through the mental and verbal abuse, now able to help someone else. Getting past that pain is not easy, but the work has been well worth it. Contrary to popular advice, I didn't get counseling right away. I took time after having my youngest son to search myself. I once heard this phrase, which rang so clear to me and sounded the alarm in my life: "Don't paint your red flags white." I had seen the red flags and allowed my selfishness, lust, fear and low self-esteem to paint them white. I didn't think I had the courage to leave. Where would I go? My parents were in another state. I didn't have a savings. My credit score was below average and I didn't have my college degree. I felt like I had no choice but to stay in the marriage. I never knew the power I had to move forward.

It was a step. One step toward saying, "Yes" to me and whatever God set in my path. I am so glad that I took the step to walk away. It was the best decision for me and my sons. In your relationships, you have to choose the path that is best for you, realizing that everyone's circumstances are different. This is a *portion* of my story. Your story may be quite different. But, either way, be true to yourself. Know who you are and find what fits you. Do not settle! Someone once said, "If you settle for less than you deserve, you will get less than what you settled for."

Do not forfeit your joy. Find you. Find freedom!

Marriage Uncut **RELOADED**
SELF-REFLECTION

1. If this story resonates with you, where do you find yourself?

   _____

   _____

2. What steps will you take to get the help you need?

   _____

   _____

3. What does emotionally and verbally abusive mean to you and are you a victim?

   _____

   _____

4. Are you taking the time to examine your relationship cycles for destructive patterns?

   _____

   _____

5. What will you do to find your truth and live out the life God has for you?

   _____

   _____

About the Author
➥ Natasha Crawford

Having been through a childhood where she lacked the love and attention from her father, and had little understanding of her worth, Natasha created some destructive relationship patterns. Being married twice has taught Natasha valuable, but costly lessons in marriage and love. Through those tough lessons, she returned to school to obtain her business degree and was determined not to let a verbally abusive marriage and divorce stop her pursuits. Natasha has three handsome, talented, intelligent boys and has since remarried the one God had for her. Natasha has matured relationally to find that love *IS* real, marriage *CAN* work if you work it, and scars *DO* heal when you deal with them.

Dr. Jekyll, Mr. Hyde
by Consuelo "Lady Coni" Hookfin

Amazing memories. Overwhelming happiness. Endless kisses. Good sex. And, of course, 1,000 happily ever after's.

That was what I had in mind about marriage when I met my Prince Charming. Among other things, he was extremely handsome, nice, tall, funny and gainfully employed. Yep, God had done a *great* job with this one! He was everything on my list, plus some. He paid for everything. He spent every day with me and bought me nice gifts. He wrote beautiful notes and spoke words to me that melted my heart like warm butter on a hot roll. And then he sang to me like I was a celebrity. I did know *that* person was Dr. Jekyll.

I was a student with a government job and was fairly debt-free with no children. I was attractive on the outside and ready for a major life change. We had only been together less than two months, but we had enough chemistry (lust) that we knew we didn't want to be apart from one another for too long. He moved back home after an Army stint and we were married about six months later. There were so many predictors of failure that day. Somehow, I just didn't pay attention to the obvious. I chose not to. My focus was solely on my man and my new life. After my parents' divorce, I felt like I was wandering around unsuccessfully, trying to discover myself. And, to be honest, I wanted love. So, a husband seemed like the logical next step.

What I thought I wanted, but really needed, would soon prove to be a stark contrast. A couple of years passed. As we started our lives together, we hit a few bumps, but nothing we couldn't handle. I saw some flashes of anger and we exchanged harsh words, but nothing too dramatic. We were supposed to last forever. But, at two years, things shifted to a much sharper dynamic.

It was after a cold work day and I was super excited to show him our daughter's first round of baby pictures. His work schedule was sort of erratic and I had asked his availability several times to go take pictures, but he hadn't given me a date. She was already two months old, so I took her to the photo studio on my own, paid for her photos and showed him the proofs.

He said, "They're really nice," but his words seemed tight and his tone was a little off.

We exchanged a few words about why I didn't wait for him so he could be in the pictures. Of course, I reminded him that I had asked him several times, but I didn't want her to get too much older without having photos. So, I decided to go myself.

"Why is it an issue? I paid for it myself."

I admit that I became a smart aleck in that moment.

"Who told you to put your big, ugly head in the pictures?" he asked. "These were *her* pictures. You didn't need to be in them."

It was such an odd statement to me.

"What mother doesn't want to take pictures with her children?"

He immediately got angry, pushed me into a corner with his hands tightly wound around my throat, and lightly cautioned me not to ever do anything with his kids if he didn't know about it first.

And that was just the beginning.

I was a little too familiar with this particular scenario. I had been in a situation with a stalker before meeting my husband. I had been physically assaulted multiple times, but I didn't realize this was something that could happen in a marriage between two people who claimed to love each other.

Through the next few years, there were several incidents of abuse – mental, physical, emotional and, worst of all, *verbal*. Bruises fade. Emotions and mindsets shift. But the power behind painful words can feel like a machine gun reverberating bullets through your chest. My heart was in pieces and there were holes everywhere.

I hadn't been taught how to properly enter a relationship with a man in a heart healthy manner. I wasn't taught how to sustain a marriage. So, the additional responsibility of children became more of a burden than a joy. That wasn't an excuse. It was just the truth. After our son was born, my husband asked me to stay home because we couldn't afford childcare for two children. Although I was apprehensive, because up until that point, I had always worked, I reluctantly agreed. We didn't talk in depth about what it meant to be at home with one income. But I figured this would be a good thing because I could give my husband more attention. Also he would feel much better about his position in our marriage since he would be the sole provider. I didn't realize that saying, "Yes" to one thing meant saying, "No" to many other things.

Our marriage was so bad that even while I was pregnant with my son, I asked God if He would just allow my body to spontaneously abort my unborn child. I promised God that I wouldn't even be mad. I didn't want a child to grow up in a home where the parents did not truly express their love to one another in a kind way. When our son was born, I didn't nurse him because I didn't want any kind of connection or bond with him. So I was at home with "the joy" of a newborn, but I didn't have any peace, personal income or any real friends. I also had to give up my new vehicle. I wasn't prepared to feel so desperately alone and neglected. My husband told me that he would give me money based on what he thought I needed.

I asked for money to go to the salon.

He said, "That's what those (relaxer) boxes are for on the shelf at the stores."

I wanted new clothes.

He said, "You're not going anywhere during the day, so why do you need any clothes?"

This situation lasted until our son went to preschool. It almost destroyed me as a saint, a woman and a *person*. One time when the kids' dad came home, he found me in the middle of the kitchen in the dark. I wasn't asleep, praying or cleaning up the floor. I was physically weak. I was literally so depressed that I felt like my mind was suspended and I couldn't move.

He said, "Well, I can't help you." Instead, he recommended that I see a psychologist because I had "so many issues" – his words. I did eventually seek professional help, but she told me that as long as I stayed in the toxic environment, her advice and guidance wouldn't help me very much. I took what I could from those sessions and tried to climb out of that deep, dark hole.

As a woman who was left emotionally wounded, torn and verbally ripped through and through, I found myself looking for consolation, support and, most of all, affirmation in places that were accessible, but actually "off limits" to me. I wanted to figure out why I felt so alone. *Was I not happy because I was holding someone else responsible for my own happiness? Was it because my husband didn't show me love? Did he not show love because he didn't love me? Did I love me? Did I accept abuse because that was my only way to feel loved? Had our marriage really been reduced to sporadic sex, no touching, little feeling and harsh, degrading conversation all the time after only four or five years?* I was so sad and disappointed in myself because I felt like I had really made a mess of things.

I finally realized *and* admitted that I was married to Mr. Hyde.

We *looked* so good together. He pastored a church and he came from a great family. We lived in a nice home and, to the outside world, we were a couple to be admired. The Bible says that the Lord will never leave us nor forsake us, but truthfully, I needed a "physical being" to be a sounding board. I wanted to "hear" someone tell me that I mattered, that I was okay. I wanted that someone to be a man, my husband. The void was so deep and the holes were so wide that I felt like if my situation didn't change soon, I was going to do something I would really regret. I was going to leave, have an affair, or commit suicide.

I didn't have a good relationship with my mother because I still felt like she was responsible for my parents' divorce. I loved my father dearly, but after the divorce, he chose a lifestyle as a homosexual, which contradicted my beliefs and went against everything he had ever taught me about God, the Bible and values. I didn't feel anything different about my father as a person, but I was hesitant about certain conversations. At the time, I did have my only sibling, with whom I had just recently reestablished a relationship. But it seemed like whenever I talked to her, she felt like many others felt: that I *wanted* to be treated badly; otherwise, I would have already left my husband. She was daring and took chances.

I wasn't.

She was pretty.

I wasn't.

She had the attention from men.

I didn't.

As we grew up, although I always made good grades, I lived in her shadow. That caused me to grow up with a complex about the meaning of true beauty and self-esteem. That complex didn't change once I got married. It got worse. I always needed affirmation, but who was going to tell me now that my husband *didn't*; well…wouldn't?

My options were limited as to whom I could talk to about my relationship. I had been isolated from my friends, so would I try talking to my husband? I did. But he always felt that no one could tell him anything. Having conversations with him made me feel so intentionally inferior. I often joked that someone of Bishop T.D. Jakes' magnitude would have to come and personally have a conversation with him before he would consider changing his ways.

I tried food to divert my loneliness, but it became my enemy. At the same time that I ate, I would turn around and starve myself. I was so angry at everything and everybody. I was also extremely depressed. Some days, I would walk to the top of the steps, but I couldn't muster up the energy to walk down. I would sob uncontrollably because I knew that meant I had to face another day with seemingly no purpose. My insides were crumbling and I was in a low place. By now, I had a vulnerability so wide in my marriage relationship that it became easy for the space to be filled with random emotional support.

The day came when this randomness materialized from a need to a thought and then, into a conversation. When I first started talking with this gentleman, I felt a connection with him at the time that I didn't feel with anyone else—including my husband. We talked a little, then we talked a little bit more. Then, we talked all the time, several times a day. The talks were centered around church and family, but they soon grew into deeper, more involved dialogue. I have never smoked crack or been addicted to alcohol. But I thought this had to be what it felt like. I wanted to hear his voice. I *needed* to hear his voice. I knew the way I felt inside was wrong, but why couldn't I talk to him? We didn't sleep together. However, morally, it was wrong because I knew deep down that there was an undeniable emotional attachment forming. Some might call it an affair. I called it a lifeline - *literally*. All these questions came up in my head about righteousness and rightness. I felt it was wrong to be neglected and mistreated, too. Sadly, somehow, I don't think I would have had them if I weren't a pastor's wife. We have problems, too. I didn't ask to be a pastor's wife. It's critical to know who and whose you are before you attach yourself to anyone else. Be truthful to yourself before you ask someone else the truth about you.

The emotional affair took wings and flew. I appreciated the benefits of being able to talk to someone whom I felt genuinely cared for me. It was convenient and easy. This person had a genuine interest in my feelings, my welfare and my life. Initially, it began with questions about how I could best please my husband. He had some insight about my husband, so I trusted his judgment. It didn't last very long because the boundaries were set early. Nonetheless, it lasted long enough for my heart to be divided. The war between my mind and heart was enough to send me into a nervous breakdown. I loved my husband, but he didn't even discern that my heart wasn't loyal, which hurt even worse. That situation ended soon enough, but not without consequence.

It was five years later when my sister and my father-in-law passed. Those two people influenced me in ways they didn't even realize. The emptiness was real. I was still trying to *make* my husband feel a certain way about me. I said things, but I knew I had to watch what I said so he wouldn't get upset. He always told me to say what I meant, but oftentimes when you are talking to a person who thinks of you negatively, you tend to reevaluate and over explain everything you do and say. I remember the times when I could literally feel my heart strings and tendons snapping. The tissue was tearing. It was at that moment that I really believed you could die from a broken heart. I remember moments when his words would paralyze me to the point that I couldn't even get in the bed. I could only lay beside the bed. I was physically weak and broken.

One of those moments was July 4, 2006. July 4th has always seemed to be a day of real fireworks—in the relationship between me and the kids' dad. At his suggestion, we sat watching a movie as another man's story brought my story to light in such a real way. Tyler Perry didn't know how many women he was writing "Diary of a Mad Black Woman" for, but he knew that God said to write it. Basically, the plot was that of a barren trophy wife who gave her heart, soul and esteem to a man who abused her. Subsequently, he cheated on her and had a child with another woman. My husband asked me to "lovingly" sit between his legs to watch the movie with him. This was when I told him that my neck was sore. I sat next to him instead and felt real uncomfortable—one, because of my neck; and two, because I could tell that was his way of trying to get close to me. I was so confused.

The memories of the evening prior stuck out in my head like someone was throwing darts on a board. Each dart that landed dismantled another piece of my heart. I was in disbelief concerning the events of this holiday because I was labeled everything from "a hoe" and "stupid" to immature and, "That's why you can't keep no man!"

It was my fault, right?

My neck was so stiff that it hurt to look down. My lower back was so sore that it was hard to sit up or sit down. My behind hurt and my wrist was twisted. My other wrist was bruised and my mind still wondered why, and how, I still loved this man who had caused me so much pain. I took a moment to reflect on the conversation that had gotten us here *this* time.

I asked him, "Will you go to a counseling session with me?"

I wanted the counselor to see what I was subjected to during times of conflict.

He immediately said, "No. You can go to a counselor to deal with *your* affair because *you* have mental problems."

He told me this while repeatedly tapping his finger on the side of my head, which made me feel like less than a person.

"Well, can we at least renew our vows since it has been 11 years?"

"You didn't keep the first ones, so why do we need to do it again?"

This was a big argument. After a while, it became so painful. I was continually reminded that I needed to say what I meant *the first time*.

He told me, "Your affair put you in this place. You need to stop crying and apologizing. Be mature about it. Go be with whomever you think can make you happy."

I backed up from him and told him, "If you had handled your business, then the emotional affair wouldn't have happened."

I knew it would make him angry, but by then, he was already so nasty to me. I wanted to hurt his feelings a little bit, too. He immediately got physical and pushed me into the shower. He was in my face and pinned me down on the floor. The weirdest part is that, although I was crying some, I was more concerned with him understanding that I wasn't trying to be a whore. My feelings were out there and I'd simply made a wrong choice. I wasn't concerned that he had my leg bent up to my neck, or that he yanked my head and my hair and pushed his fingers into my eyes so I would look at him. I also wasn't thinking about the fact that he kept hitting my head into the floor and slapping my face. I was trying to get my point across.

He said, "You're trying to act like the man! That's why you keep getting up off the floor!"

After this was over, it was difficult to walk. However, I was still trying to run behind him and trying to make him see that I was not accusing him of not forgiving me. The worst thought from the day prior was probably that I felt it was alright for him to hit me because I knew he needed to vent.

He said, "I can't help you. Only God can. You were messed up long before you trapped me into this marriage."

Even if all these things were true, is it necessary to say it in this way that is so cruel?

Mr. Hyde.

I asked him, "Why shouldn't I cry?"

He said, "You lack maturity. I can't talk to you because you're not mature. You have tantrums like a little kid. The only reason you cry is because the truth hurts."

During this argument, I asked him, "How could you possibly be a pastor and over people, but talk to me like that?"

He repeatedly said, "Coni, you said you wanted to talk, and now look. You can put it out, but you can't take it."

It's important for us to understand that as humans what's deep-seeded in us comes out in various ways in our interactions with each other. Others' actions reveal certain things in us that we don't know still exist within, like anger, depression and unforgivenness. When you, or someone you are in a relationship with, closes off their intimate side to you, that need doesn't go away. It causes you to be open and vulnerable to other things that meet the need for intimacy. It's important to seal even the smallest cracks.

If my marriage was going to survive, I needed to give him more time to sort it all out. I tried to convince myself that he was just mean and/or going through a rough time, but he really loved me. It's the lie you tell yourself so you don't have to face reality.

I would routinely ask, "If you feel so terrible about me as a person, why do we stay together?"

His reply, "I never asked you to stay; this is *my* house, Coni!"

I apologized for making him upset.

His response was, "Man, Coni. I am sorry for everything that just happened, but you just need to use wisdom and learn what to say when you want to talk."

The apology did seem genuine. He even kissed me and we later had sex. I just wanted everything to be okay. One of the effects of narcissistic treatment is the ability to transfer blame to yourself and internalize everything. I told myself that it was all my fault and that I didn't stand up for myself. It was my fault that I started discussions without thinking of how they may end up. It was my fault that I settled for this marriage as a definition of love. It was my fault that I subjected my children to the effects of our arguments when my demeanor was sad and I didn't want to talk. It was my fault that I didn't love myself and want better for myself. Often, people judge harshly because they haven't experienced such levels of depression and their mental health is strong. But you can get to a place mentally where you feel there is no hope. If you stay in that place for too long, you can become disillusioned. It's imperative to self-check and stay focused.

I was so disappointed, sad and horrified that two saved, married adults carried on in this way that was totally unpleasing to God. The next day, Dr. Jekyll showed up.

He said, "I'm sorry. We are at a crossroads. We have to look at it like it is a test. I'm tired of the cycle we are in. We have to decide if we have had enough. If we can't make it, we can go our separate ways. My biggest weakness is that I don't respect or value you as a first lady. You bring out a lot of bad in me. No one could do that, but you."

Of all the physical interactions we'd had to date, this was the second worst. That was a time I shared some of my feelings. He responded, "You just should have said that you wanted me to show you some love! I am not going to be put on the defensive; otherwise you will get a bad result."

We talked for a while. He told me that he felt like a dog. He didn't feel like one of God's servants because he realized that it really got out of hand. Unfortunately, he and I were never able to get on the same page at the same time. I felt like I was teaching my kids to bury their heads in the sand, as if nothing had happened, which is dangerous and toxic.

There were several situations that caused me to reconsider my place in his life and my own. We separated after 18 years. If I didn't know him in marriage, I certainly didn't know him in separation. I subsequently filed for divorce a year later. My health was affected in ways that I couldn't even understand. Never believe that your body doesn't know and respond to trauma and pain. I started early menopause, which was confirmed by labs. I had the urge to urinate often, but couldn't seem to empty my bladder. I developed migraines and my face broke out repeatedly. On the day I picked up the divorce papers, I went to the bathroom and found spontaneous bleeding. I nearly hyperventilated when I left the attorney's office. I had chest pains and I couldn't catch my breath. I was crying uncontrollably, all while trying to drive. My heart literally hurt. I felt like I was ending someone else's life, but that was just the beginning.

November 2014. We sat. We swore. And we agreed that, after 20 years, no more. In eleven short minutes, "divorced" became my new last name. The transition was brutal because I never thought I'd be divorced. I thought the separation would last about three months and he would realize my value to his life. But everything that was bad became worse. *Everything!* Remember: Stay true to you! Live in reality. It will help you make better decisions about your life. In a family situation, if you aren't emotionally healthy, those around you likely won't be.

That seems like it was a lifetime ago, even though it has only been five years. I realize that if I hadn't left, I would have died either by his hand or mine. I had to leave to find me. I also went through the five stages of grief several times. You have to allow yourself to "feel" each emotion; otherwise, you will stunt your own growth. I was able to navigate through missing him; missing my family; missing the feeling of being married; missing the companionship; missing the church and other entities attached to the marriage; missing my in-laws; missing our mutual friends; missing the actual security of the marriage and many other aspects associated with the family unit. Thank God that I made it through because failure in any of these areas can cause you not to recover well or at all.

Seek peace and pursue it. The joy of "new and true peace" can't be compared to anything else. May you find peace and be peace in your life. God created the body in a miraculous way to heal itself. This journey I am on is simply amazing. I feel better than ever from the inside out. The recovery process of building your "life after" will cost you mind, body, soul and spirit, but it will be worth every second and the self-awareness is priceless.

I am an advocate for love and I believe that marriage is one of God's miracles, waiting to happen between two amazing people. No one but God can do what is necessary to cause change in the heart of a man. The difference in my thought process now is that I love *me* first and my boundaries are safely in place. All things new!

> *You intended to harm me,*
> *but God intended it all for good.*
> *He brought me to this position so*
> *I could save the lives of many people.*
> –Genesis 50:20 (NLT)

Marriage Uncut RELOADED
SELF-REFLECTION

1. If you knew then what you know now about you, what would you change about how you choose relationship partners?

   _____
   _____
   _____
   _____

2. How important is it to seek professional help after trauma?

   _____
   _____
   _____
   _____

3. Does your spouse need to know secrets about you before or after marriage? If so, what secrets?

   _____
   _____
   _____
   _____

About the Author
➥ Coni Hookfin

The redefining moment for Coni Hookfin life's was turning 40. She realized that although she was alive, she had not yet lived. The spirit in her reminded her that she was born with purpose, but it wouldn't be fulfilled if she "died in the middle". Her ministries were birthed out of matters of the heartbreak that nearly destroyed her, but she is a picture perfect reflection of the process of release, restoration and recovery!

She wholeheartedly believes that everyone has the ability to reinvent themselves, which is a privilege from God. With the start of each new day, she knows firsthand that we are all given the opportunity to do at least one thing differently than we did the day before. She encourages others to write the vision so they can see it before they see it. As a smart, nurturing and intuitive woman of God, Coni loves to sing, write, read and create scrapbooks. She knows that her future will consist of major event planning, recording a chart-topping album, publishing several bestselling books and manuals, and continuing to obtain wholeness, which equals true happiness. Her advice to everyone she encounters is to stop wishing, and *start doing*.

About
So It Is Written, LLC

 We are a full-service content writing and editorial company, designed to assist with your every need as it relates to the written word. Writing and editing can be extremely time consuming. The words on your website, in your book or on your professional resume are crucial to your overall success. They can make or break you. But, we can help!

So It Is Written, LLC believes in the quality of the written word and drafting content in excellence. Whether it's content for the web, brochures, editing manuscripts for bestselling authors or ghostwriting for the author who just doesn't have the time to complete his/her manuscript, we have what it takes to fulfill your literary needs.

Call us at 313-999-6942 today or email info@soitiswritten.net for more details about our personalized writing and editing services. We look forward to working with you to make your project one of excellence!

About
The Red Ink Conference

The Red Ink Conference Known as the Premier Conference for authors, editors, playwrights and more, this writing conference empowers attendees from around the nation to write, edit and market their next bestseller in excellence. Many of the attendees are indie authors who are just starting their publishing journey. We're inviting aspiring bestsellers, as well as those who want to take their writing to the next level by editing for other indie authors, to join us in this year in one of two locations–or both! Our expert presenters have over 20 years of industry experience and run successful businesses that support indie authors nationwide. We're excited to make a dent in the book publishing world and have our attendees learn new, innovative information that will position them to build a solid platform as an author and speaker. For more information, visit theredinkconference.com.

www.ingramcontent.com/pod-product-compliance
Lightning Source LLC
Chambersburg PA
CBHW050437010526
44118CB00013B/1562